Foreword by: Daniela Roman
International Bestselling Author

Where's Mom?

Against All Odds
Making the Most of Single Parenthood

By: Jannette Ramos, MSW
AWARD-WINNING AUTHOR

Where's Mom?
Against All Odds
Making the Most of Single Parenthood

Copyright © 2020 by Jannette Ramos, MSW

All rights reserved by the author. No part of this book may be used or reproduced or transmitted in any form or by any electronic means including photocopying, recording, or by storage in any retrieval system without the written permission from the author.

Disclaimer
The contents of this book should be used for information only. The author, affiliate organizations and publisher assume no responsibility for any decision made as a result of reading this book that can affect your business or personal life.

1st Printing

ISBN: 978-1-7343699-1-5

Printed in the United States of America

QUOTES

"It is easier to build strong children than to repair broken men."

Frederick Douglass

"The best way to make children good is to make them happy."

Oscar Wilde

"Tired as a mother."

Unknown

"Children need your presence more than your presents."

Jesse Jackson

"Never be afraid to fail as a mother, it's actually better because you don't lose, you learn!" Children are lifelong lessons

Jannette Ramos, MSW

"If you want blessings, be one!

Author Unknown

Table of Contents

QUOTES 7
FOREWORD 11
TESTIMONIALS 15
ACKNOWLEDGMENTS 17
INTRODUCTION 21
CHAPTER I: My Life Raising Two Males 23
CHAPTER II: Child's Love 33
CHAPTER III: Sacrifice 41
CHAPTER IV: Time 49
CHAPTER V: Adolescence 57
CHAPTER VI: Lifelong Memories 67
CHAPTER VII: Solitude Effects 73
CHAPTER VIII: Rewards 79
CHAPTER IX: Second Chance 85
CHAPTER X: Final Thoughts Take Care of Yourself ... 93
RESOURCES 97

FOREWORD

As a young, naive and inexperienced eighteen-year old, I trusted people too easily which led me to my first abusive relationship with my life spiraling out of control from there. Being sexually assaulted at nineteen while I slept left me traumatized for nearly thirty years.

It wasn't until I met my husband, Emilio, that I learned all about forgiveness and letting go. Every child deserves the unconditional love only a mother can bring. Forgiving helped the healing process. In turn, it helped me to realize my story needed to be shared to help other young women in similar situations.

My first co-authorship, Magnetic Entrepreneur For Women Leadership, by Robert J. Moore, from Canada, gave me the platform to begin sharing my message. The response I received was amazing! He taught me forgiveness wasn't for the other person;

Words can't begin to explain how it made me feel. Improving someone's life in a positive way is very powerful, yet humbling.

As an advocate for women, and as someone who endured two abusive relationships, helping young women break away from emotionally and physically abusive relationships is both my mission and my passion.

My husband, Emilio introduced me to Jannette. They both grew up in Camden, New Jersey, a city, in spite of its economic struggles and history of violence, is a city of a rich diversity of cultures, where hard working families are always willing to foster their family traditions and good will for their community.

After meeting Jannette at a local park one day, I felt an immediate connection to her. After hearing her story of being a single mom, I was inspired. Her story is one of strength, courage and determination. After becoming a young mom, she unfortunately lost the support of her husband. He was struggling with a drug addiction and really wasn't there for her or their children.

I admire Jannette's endurance to try and make her marriage work but ultimately, she could no longer put her boys in harm's way due to their father's continued risky lifestyle. Finally, they decided the marriage needed to end, and they had to move on alone.

Returning to her hometown of Camden, New Jersey was not easy, but was necessary for Janette to raise her children. The love Jannette has for her boys is stronger than any challenge she would face, and it drove her even more to provide them with the best life possible.

Jannette has been working with social services for over twenty years seeing more than her fair share of family tragedies and crisis. She is dedicated to helping families in need and in similar situations to the one she herself was once in. Being an advocate for her community and doing whatever possible to reach out and assist in any way is her mission.

Soon after speaking with Jannette, we knew she would be a perfect fit for our second edition of our Spiritual Fitness Survivor book. This co-authorship shares people's stories of survival. Jannette told us she had always wanted to write a book and share her amazing story. It didn't take her long to agree to be a part of this wonderful collaboration. Her story is in chapter 15 and Jannette is now an Award-Winning Author!

After having the experience writing her chapter and being honored at our book launch with an award and certificate of courage, Jannette knew she now had an obligation to take it one step further. Today, she has lived out her dream and written her complete story in this beautiful book. We are convinced after reading her story you will see what my husband and I saw. Jannette is the true representative of a woman who never gave up, no matter how difficult or challenging life became.

She made many sacrifices on her journey to provide and always be there for her boys. She has proven when you have children; you do whatever it takes to give them the life they deserve. Now the proud mother of two incredible young men who are living very successful and productive lives, she knows all the hard work she did has paid off.

Most importantly, Jannette wants to express how instrumental it is to have your mother in your life. It goes without saying a father is important and needed in a child's upbringing as well. But there is a very special connection from the moment of conception between a mother and a child. We as women, nurture, feed, and love this amazing creation every second and every step of the way until the moment they are born into this world. That bond only grows stronger from then on. There is nothing like a mom's hug, touch, or shoulder to cry on when you fall or after your first heartbreak. Nothing can ever tear that special bond apart. This is the message this strong, beautiful and resilient mother wants everyone to be aware of. She has proven when you have children; you do whatever it takes to give them the life they deserve. Most importantly, no child should ever have to grow up asking "Where's Mom?"

> *"A mother is she who can take the place of all others but whose place no one else can take."*
>
> **Cardinal Mermillod**

TESTIMONIALS

"She loves children!" Her own and the children she works with. She is a special person!

Kenneth Fowlkes

"Jannette is an inspiration! A true testament to motherhood and courage"
God bless.

Gary Farnesi
Director of Commercial Lending
WSFS Bank

I have known Jannette for 17 years. She has always been passionate about her children and making sure they were on the "right path of life."

Lisa Capone, MSW

I have known the Author, Jannette Ramos and her two (2) boys Luis and Daniel since 2004. As a single parent "she gets it." Far too often single parents don't understand the importance of sacrifice and putting the needs of their children first. Jr. raised two boys into outstanding men while living in a city that at one time was considered the most dangerous city in the country. Jr. is an advocate for education and rather than chose public schools she paid tuition so that her boys would receive a great education. She chose the education of her boys over anything personal or materialistic for herself.

Lance Saunders, BA

I've known Jannette for almost 10 years, I've watched her make numerous sacrifices doing a phenomenon job raising two of the best young men who I've ever had the presence of being in their lives. Jannette is the new TIGER MOM.

She raises men not boys.

Jannette should have a patent on the words, Presence not Presents in children's lives. 💪👍☺

Regards,
Steve Potter

ACKNOWLEDGMENTS

First and foremost, I thank God for allowing me to achieve this and giving me the opportunity to share my story with the world! Although we have free will to do whatever we choose to, he will guide you in the right direction each time you want to make positive differences and changes to salvage families!

My two adult sons, Luis Echevarria and Daniel Echevarria! You two represent my reasons for living and when times were tough, seeing your smiles and happiness just to be around me, gave me the inspiration to strive to be the best mother I could be! I didn't give YOU the gift of Life, Life gave ME the gift of YOU! I love you both to the moon and back!

To my current partner Bernardo Campusano, I value and appreciate the support and love you have provided me during this time. Thank you for rooting for me and just being there and providing me with the tools I needed to make this book reality. You are the "behind the scenes" that made this project move forward. I am a lucky woman!

To my mother Maria Ramos and my siblings; Carmen, Maritza, Nancy, Angel, Javier and David who although we don't always see each other daily, you have each been a help, support, an influence in my life, and have been there in some form or fashion.

To all those men whom I dated and just didn't make the cut to help me raise my children. Thank you as this was my path to raise them on my own.

To my co-worker and counselor Jose Carrero Reyes. The number of times I have swarmed your office talking about all I would be accomplishing in life and you never turned me away or complained. You have been there to give me reason, great advice and just to listen. I am forever grateful!

To my two good friends Jenny Loebelle and Carmen Soto who were there while I was raising my two children and gave me the best advice on how to care for them. Your friendship is priceless and I am forever grateful.

To Steve Potter, Lance Saunders, Ed Lopez and Al Buck who were there to give me advice during the years Luis and Daniel were growing up. You encouraged me to believe in myself and had some form of bonding with Luis and Daniel! You four will never be forgotten for your faith, motivation, and support you gave me!

To DCP&P employment for allowing me to financially support my children.

To my long-term working peers, Lisa Capone, Denise Goodnow, Dennise Mateo, and all of my other working partners, who go tired of hearing me talk about my children.

To Emilio Roman and his beautiful wife Daniela Roman. Emilio, that day I prayed to continue my book after having written it a few years before, you were the one calling out to give me the inspiration on why this needed to happen. Thank you both for believing in me and giving me the motivation to just move forward!

To Laurie K. Grant from SHYUI Digital Transformations, thank you for your magic in birthing my book to life.

Thank you all!
Jannette Ramos, MSW

INTRODUCTION

This book was written for you, the single parent (mother) who doesn't know that the life and direction of her child is in her hands. Nobody ever said raising children would be easy! It's Not! But the crucial part in raising children is to be part of their lives. Children need YOU to be there...to listen, to care, to help, to guide, to mold, to redirect, to teach, to love unconditionally, and to build who they are going to become as adults in tomorrow's world! How do I know this? I am a mother of two now adult sons!

I not only had the privilege of having been blessed with two wonderful adults' males, but to see what they have become and developed into, is the best rewards and outcome any mother could ask for. It wasn't easy but it can be done. Not having the best of everything and major sacrifices went into this, but it was well worth every ounce of effort, moves, lack of sleep, aches and pains, joys, and strengths to build the men they are today.

This book is intended to inspire any single mother who thinks they cannot do this on their own, who feels like they cannot care or raise their children. You can do it!!!

Against all odds, against what society may say and think! You can do it! Making a commitment is part of this. Children need their mothers! It's just that simple! They will have a better chance in life knowing there is no void to fill. The key is never to give up and take care of yourself. Please remember children don't stay "little" forever...Your breaks and rewards will come one day!

Be inspired, be ready, and be the mother you were intended to be in this world! Your children will appreciate it and will reward you in the end! Stay strong!!!

CHAPTER I:
My Life Raising Two Males

Jannette Ramos, MSW

"Children need your presence more than your presents."

Jesse Jackson

To BE or NOT to be? That was my question when I pondered about writing my life! Everyone has a story to tell, and ONE is never too old to tell it! I want to be an influence on someone's life by writing my story in hopes of making a change in their life. For someone who has gone or is undergoing something similar, I have chosen to BE!

My life begins at a young age of sixteen when I decided it was time to leave my home because I thought I was ready to become an adult! We all feel like that especially when trying to escape a life of poverty, domestic violence, and problems. We think this will become resolved by the mere escape of leaving home at a young age.

I married at the age of seventeen and left the State of New Jersey for the unfamiliar state of Connecticut. Waterbury, Connecticut; a place of hilly roads, cold winters, and mountains. As I began to embark on the life of a married woman, I thought I wanted; I found out the life I sought was only a dream. Mr. E led a chosen life of drugs, specifically heroin.

This was not easy to accept since he was no longer the person I had married. As a result, the life I was living brought many tears, anger, and anxiety. I didn't know what I was going to do and how daily life was going to end up being. There were times I was

Where's Mom?

hungry, alone and scared as I didn't know who this person was. I felt betrayed and yet empowered! I was mature at a young age. This would bring me to make decisions about where my life would lead. I could have chosen the path of drugs, risking losing myself and my children, but I managed to stay FOCUSED AND DETERMINED!

This life caused tension and distance as the times worsened. I managed to remain in the relationship as one is taught to remain invested in marriage and where was I to go? Back home? And be reminded my marriage was a failure? I wasn't ready for that! I wasn't ready for the confrontation, and I already had one child who needed me! Needless to say; I stayed in the relationship to seek answers and solutions to these real problems. Unfortunately, that didn't happen.

There were times when a knock on the door informed me Mr. E was incarcerated for stealing, was high when he got to the home or was so sick he could barely stand. Then there were those times he was so high his eyes changed, he had the smell of copper on his skin, picking his skin and eating candy as if it was water. I didn't know what drugs were, as I was an innocent youth who had not been raised around illegal substances. It was difficult for me to comprehend the changes initially. Soon, I became an expert and could spot those behaviors from miles away.

Two years into the marriage, I became pregnant and had my first son Luis on October 22nd, 1991 whom I patiently and excitedly waited for as he came into this world. The first child is always a great excitement, and I wanted to be the perfect mother. I delivered on my own without any fatherly support in the hospital room. As time goes on, I am taking care of my child and trying to be the best mother I can. Little did I know throughout the first year of my child's life, Mr. E had impregnated another young lady who had her child two months before I had my son! I was torn apart!

However, I managed to maintain the relationship as I wanted a family. Mr. E. tried ways of getting clean which included drug rehabilitation, cold turkey, and other forms with no success. Ultimately, he always managed to take the last twenty dollars available to go get HIGH. I was not on drugs and feeling the effects of poverty, pain, and no way out of this situation.

I worked to pass the time and survive as best as I could, but I needed to be educated. I went back to college to empower myself while trying to make a healthier life for my son. Somehow, I was able to secure low-income housing while going back to school and working. I inherited support from a neighbor who was able to care for my child while I worked. This helped a lot!

In spite of my situation, I was willing to make it work and the relationship dragged for a few years! By this time, four years have gone by, and it happens again! I became pregnant, I was very excited; yet saddened as my life hasn't changed for the better in the relationship! I realized I needed to find a life that was going to benefit myself and the children. I couldn't

Where's Mom?

remain in this dysfunction forever! I was too smart, getting educated and wanting a safe and secure loving home.

I delivered on December 3rd, 1996, an eight-pound baby boy naming him Daniel. As I waited for his brother to arrive at the hospital to meet his sibling, I can vividly remember Mr. E appeared to be under the influence of heroin. I was disheartened and angry that he would risk the life of "my child" being high.

A month went by and the DECISION FINALLY CAME to leave the relationship. I was back at work within a week of delivering my baby. I had no choice! I had no money! I don't remember how I got home from work that afternoon, but when I did, neither of my children were there! I was upset, anxious, and angry! After some time, they entered the door with, guess what, Mr. E being high!

I decided that day (**YES, THAT DAY**) I was NOT going to be in a relationship any longer. I was done!!! How could a person on drugs take my children to buy drugs and risk their lives? I would have not forgiven myself if ANYTHING had happened to those children.

I returned to Camden, New Jersey, in February 1997. I can vividly remember that day still in Connecticut. Aside from consoling my four-year-old who didn't want to leave, I had yanked my big toenail in the entrance of a McDonalds (Ouch did that hurt!!!) I should mention Mr. E at this time was incarcerated for stealing and trying to sustain his heroin habit. However, this was a regular for him as he needed to feed his "addiction!"

Jannette Ramos, MSW

> *I've been a depressed mom. A sad mom. A happy mom. A mad mom. A mean mom. A drained mom. A broke mom. A stable mom. An unstable mom. But I've tried my best to be there, no matter what.*
>
> ***Author Unknown***

Tough days lay ahead for a young single mother with two children who they relied on financially. I had bills to pay; the children to feed and aspirations to get ahead in life! My drive to be an independent person and provide for my children, sent me back to school to obtain a Bachelor's Degree and Master's Degree in Social Work.

School and employment did not prevent me from daily interaction with my children. They were my inspiration in life!!! I gave them my time, attention, focus, love, interaction, food, guidance, direction, and skills to be who they are today! The "Three Musketeers" as I have always called us, have been my inspiration and drive in life to be who I am today!

Today I see and reap the benefits of having been there for my children REGARDLESS of what life dished out and the tough situations! I didn't quit nor did I get influenced by others to go down the wrong paths! This could have easily been my outcome if I had not been strong and had a good upbringing by my own mother. In the city of Camden, where the statistics indicate you're a product of your environment and you will fail, I am here to say this is not the case! I am not of the stereotypical view that says I will be a failure! I can honestly say it is NOT the environment

Where's Mom?

of where one lives, but rather the dedication a mother/parent provides a child.

I thank God for the "sane brain" at a very young age to be able to make decisions that would benefit my children and myself! Our children are borrowed and as mothers, we are here to provide them with the tools needed to help guide their way into life! Our children deserve that and more! Having a mother in my life influenced me greatly to make decisions and be a good mother.

This is the KEY to raising children, whether with or without another parent! It is not about material things, what you seek, or how much money in the world you have. It's about self-identity and belonging to a circle of another life. Your life starts with mom! Your children need identity, and they need to know their roots! It starts with the upbringing and sacrifices of a mother and it is PRICELESS! Birthdays, awards, riding a bike, getting sick, attending sports, helping with homework, acknowledgment and assurance that all will be ok is NEEDED while a child is growing up. Children need one person who will love them UNCONDITIONALLY!

This is not to say there are exceptions in life as THERE ARE! Having both parents raising their child/ren is OUTSTANDING however for those situations where this cannot occur the presence of a mother is needed! And a mother CAN raise children on her own! Children need to be raised by their mothers to ultimately lead healthy lives. Mothers play a vital role in ensuring their child grows up to be a "functional" or "normal" human being. Her day to day interactions with her children are what makes them who they become and how they treat others. Children need to be attended to. As mothers, we SHOULD sacrifice ourselves for the betterment of our offspring! I am not saying this is easy as it is not, but it can be done!

To this end, I am here to tell you – YOU CAN DO IT!! It is a sacrifice, but there is a reason we are here on earth to …SACRIFICE OURSELVES for our children's future! Don't give up on your children! They don't stay infants forever and all you do will influence their lives, well-being, and the rewards you will receive in the future! Here's to your child's FUTURE! Remember this, although we have different journeys in life, the DESTINATION should be the same for ALL human beings!!! Our children want their identity and to belong.

Raising awareness to all the MOTHERS who think they cannot do this on their own…You can! Will you be one of the ones who sacrifice all she has for her children or will you be one of those mothers whose child or children are asking WHERE'S MOM?

> *"There can be no keener revelation of a society's soul than the way in which it treats its children."*
>
> **Nelson Mandela,**
> **Former President of South Africa**

CHAPTER II:
Child's Love

Jannette Ramos, MSW

A child needing love from his mother is one of the most critical aspects in the world! It is necessary and it is warranted! There is no sugar coating the love from a mother! From the moment of conception, there is an unbreakable bond between a mother and her baby! That number one love only progresses through time. How you nurture that love, is completely vital to the raising of your child. Children don't ask to be brought into this life! As a mother, it is your responsibility to love your child! No matter what! There isn't any negotiation; you have an obligation as a parent to love your children.

How do you love a child when you weren't loved or raised by a parent especially a mother? This is a tough question as love develops with time. It is challenging to demonstrate something you haven't been given. However, its innate in us to do so. For example, we can pick out a comfortable shirt or shoe we like and learn to love it as we continue to use it. We begin to get comfortable and content knowing that comfort is going to be there and make us happy. Although the love of a child is not comparable to the love of a shirt or shoe, it serves the purpose of demonstrating how one goes from liking to loving. As human beings, we have the capability of what we know as "love."

Let's talk about love and its significance. To give you the text book or dictionary version of what the word means. LOVE is:

1. An intense feeling of deep affection.
2. A great interest and pleasure in something.
3. A person or thing that one loves.

Although many terms can be used, it is a hard term to define but for the purposes of children, love is something that progresses through the time and is the attention a mother provides. But where or who do we get it from? Our family, our friends, our animals, society, our environment, or is it the first source of who brings us into this world; to life...our mother? Is it safe to say the love of a mother comes from inception? We know a mother carries a fetus for nine months (give or take during a normal pregnancy.) Those months of bonding, connection, togetherness, peace, knowledge and preparation knowing your baby is going to be a boy or a girl, has both a mixture of happiness and doubt as your child is about to be born.

CONGRATULATIONS!! Or should it be my condolences as this is the beginning of what a child's life whether it be a normal productive life or a dysfunctional one? The idea here is from the moment a child is born and how much love he or she will be given is a determining factor of who he or she will be throughout his or her life!

Children are brought into this world not knowing what the fate of their life is going to be. Some of them won't be able to experience a normal life because of a breakdown throughout their childhood/adolescent life. This is the hand of fate as we have no choice in whom our mother is going to be! Who determines that you ask? I don't have the answer to this particular question. However, I do know that unfortunately who you are born from depending on what transpired in their life, will offset what happens to yours. Thus, raising several questions from lives such as: What happened? Where did the love go?

Where was the breakdown and questions are asked such as "Why couldn't mom love me enough to keep me around?" "Was I not good enough?" "What could have prevented her from giving me up?" "How can this be fixed or prevented?" "Will I get or have a second chance?" "Can I heal from this?" "Can this relationship be salvaged?" "Where's mom?"

Although I don't and have never discounted a father's role in a child's life, a mother's role is inexplicable! It is unconditional and it serves a purpose that will never be replaced, matched, or surpassed! There is something about a mother's role and love that doesn't come close to a male or father's role. We are all provided with a concept of love. It starts from infancy…the bonding a mother formulates with her child happens because women are innately wired to bond. It's supposed to be normal and functional. Whatever you choose to believe, whether it's through God's doing or through evolution, the same holds truth to the relationship that builds a child's safety, trust and connection toward a female.

This very same female is supposed to guide a child through their first eighteen years of life. I said eighteen years because currently society establishes a child going from an infant to adult in that time period. There have been many studies regarding the importance of a mother's role as it relates to the special bonding and love she provides her child. What she does in her child's life matters! She has to be there and play a vital role in her child's life! This is NOT just me writing this to say! It's TRUE!

Where's Mom?

As you read this, think about your life and upbringing as to who was there. Was it a mother, father, grandmother, aunt or uncle, friend or even yourself? Think about what that upbringing has done to your life. What roles did each one hold in your life? Why? Was your mother absent? Were you lacking female connection? Did it make you angry toward your mother? Do you see her today? Do you speak to her? How has this affected your life? What do you remember in her absence that you question or want to ask her today? Are you living a normal life or have you struggled somehow? Was or is your life dysfunctional? Was there Chaos? Did you experience an uncertainty, were you in a gang, defiant, used drugs, sold drugs, served time in jail, have had terrible and dysfunctional relationships? Are your decisions today affected by her input? Why or why not? Has her absence caused you to make stupid decisions? What would you say to her if you saw her? Would you forgive her?

Those questions were formulated not to make you angry or sad about your situation, but mainly to acknowledge how "powerful" and "deep" the absence of a mother affects one's life. If you could have one person in your life who has been missing, who would it be? I hope if you ask this question and seek an honest answer, you would have said your mother! A mother's role is "Irreplaceable!" It just is...

Let me also add it is the bare principal to a young child's future success in adulthood. A mother's involvement will more likely than not, be a key success in her child's life. Since a mother is the principal candidate to a child's upbringing and success, she must be part of the child's life...I mean really involved! It's not just being there physically with your child, but being DEVOTED! It is more than just being there physically; she needs to be "present" with her children.

A mother's role is much more than just knowing your child is alive! It's the day in and day out of a child's life! It's the knowing the who, what, where, when and why of a child's life! Being a mother is more than just having a baby! Motherhood is about TIME - the time you give to your child. Any fertile female can birth a baby; however, a mother provides all the unconditional love without knowing what the future holds in store for her child. Why is it, some mothers have children, and not only lack love, but they don't want or know how to love their children? They don't provide them with the time and attention they need and require? Where does this breakdown come from? What happened to them in their own lives? Do you see the principal? Can you see the point in how a mother's love and time is so vital to the life of a child, a teenager, and as an adult? Is it history repeating itself? Has this happened before? Can this be cured or corrected? Can the curse be broken? These are the questions a woman should be asking herself before having children as the decision has a grave impact on yours and your child's life.

CHAPTER III:
Sacrifice

Jannette Ramos, MSW

In our lives, we have all been forced to sacrifice. When we think of sacrificing, it sounds like a "negative" position that many don't want to endure. When we sacrifice something or someone, we feel as if we lose out. Ultimately, a sacrifice is giving up something or someone for the gain of something or someone else. It doesn't necessarily have to be a "bad" or negative thing. Sacrifices are required daily and for the sake of a positive change or outcome and who wouldn't make that decision?

As parents, especially mothers; our sacrifices come at the time we choose to accept becoming a mother. It is at that very moment that sacrifices begin taking place. It means we have selfishly or selflessly, have made the bold decision about doing or not doing anything. You decide at that very moment what the decision is and how it is going to affect you. For example, if one is a social drinker and decides to sacrifice drinking for the sake of saving their lives, then this is a huge sacrifice. If you choose to sacrifice your liver and continue to drink, then again, it's a sacrifice. One chooses how huge or tiny a sacrifice can become with motherhood.

Sacrificing yourself for the sake of raising your child is the "ultimate sacrifice." It's a life-long decision your children will acknowledge and appreciate in their adult lives. Sacrificing for a positive outcome will bring you so many rewards and happiness! This is not going to be a sacrifice in vain nor is it a small one! Becoming a mother is the biggest decision but is not to be taken lightly. However, once the decision is made, it shouldn't be undone or revised! What causes mothers to undo their sacrifices of raising their children? I don't have the answers to all the questions or the reasons, but my principle opinion is once you make the decision to have a child and be a mother, you sacrifice yourself for your child/ren.

Let's keep it real and clear, once you have a baby, it is not about "YOU" any longer! Many of your wants, desires, and aspirations will have to be placed on "hold." I am not saying once you become a mother you lose yourself or your livelihood, but your life will need to revolve around your children. It must be focused on your children for them to secure a better chance in society! Your sacrifice depends on their outcomes in life! I didn't make up this rule nor is it something I am making up for the sake of saying! Look at the world around you today and see what has been occurring because a mother is not involved in her child's life. The foundation you provide your child matters!

You have to as a mother have other priorities in your life which include focusing your "time" and "energy" on your children. They will rely on you for many things and need you to take the lead! You are their basis of life and their link to a sane and productive life! All or most all of the decisions made in their lives are or will be a reflection of what they were taught and shown by you! You are their guiding light! They need you to be there to help them find themselves. It's the ultimate sacrifice you give them! A sacrifice all for the betterment of their lives! This was your choice to have them! Even if it wasn't your choice initially, it was decided you would bring an innocent human life into this world! They did not ask to be here! But here they are and without instructions on how to be cared

Jannette Ramos, MSW

for which makes it even more difficult! I totally understand. I went through this on my own, and my sacrifice was their foundation for a better life! Sacrifice...a deep, rooted, and long-life changing world!

A commitment to another human being who didn't ask to be a part of our world but was destined to come here. Do you think if many mothers knew what the ultimate sacrifice of raising children was going to be like, they would do it? Would there be fewer humans in the world? Would there be less crime, poverty, hate, gang involvement, drug involvement, homelessness...etc.?

One can ponder on the answers; however, it doesn't negate the fact that as a direct result of the lack of a mother's sacrifices, we have so much in this world proving how necessary a mother's involvement in the raising of her children must be. If mothers made the necessary sacrifices, so much could result in different directions and outcomes... This is not about you! It's time to wake up and carry out the sacrifices you need to make as a mother to RAISE YOUR CHILDREN because you made the decision to bring them into the world.

The decision to ensure children are being raised by their mothers, not their grandmothers, aunts, sisters, friends, or anyone else is most important! Please don't misunderstand the points in this theory, I'm not saying there won't be cases where other women will be raising someone else's children! It's evident that through cases like death, mental health, drug addicted mothers, cases of citizenship, some other

Where's Mom?

female is going to intervene to raise that child. There will always be a percentage of children whose lives will have no other choice than to go to someone else! Their mothers won't raise them because they cannot!

However, in most other cases, MOTHERS need to be raising their own children whether it be with the support of a father, husband, grandmother, friend or anyone else they choose to help them! It is their ultimate sacrifice to raise their own children the "best" way they know possible! I don't know what the best "way" is to from one family to another family as they are all different. As a result, all upbringings are different as it relates to culture, teachings, learned behaviors, trial and error, readings, parenting books and experiences. The KEY point here is that the woman who has this child, baby, fetus in her womb for about nine months, who has created this immense bonding (yes, in the womb), who has made the decision to keep her baby, who has sacrificed herself for the life of her child, carries out the sacrifice of attending, raising, protecting, teaching, modeling, loving and guiding her children! That decision was made and the sacrifice holds and glues to that decision. A decision which impacts a child's life.

It's your responsibility and you owe it to your child! You were provided with an opportunity to raise a child in your care for the next eighteen years! To make a child into a productive, sane, independent, responsible, whole male or female is what you as their mother has been given the option to make. The sacrifice of having to let yourself go on things you wouldn't traditionally do or haven't done because you were childless but are now are required to do, go out the window because children come first! They are tomorrow's doctors, lawyers, entrepreneurs, teachers, engineers, and police! The men and women who gain a more significant chance at life because of your sacrifice!

A sacrifice which will result in less loss, unkindness, dysfunctional relationships, deaths, turmoil, crime, fighting, more respect for females and more unity! Until the cycle of missing mothers is disrupted, will the chaos of children's lives cease to exist! Children have to be raised by their mothers for this to work! The world will not be purified of the disasters that besiege us on a daily basis due to the missing "link" or sacrifice not made! The world will become a better place to live in when mothers maintain the sacrifice of being mothers! For their sake, the sake of their children's lives and the sake of humanity!

CHAPTER IV:
Time

Jannette Ramos, MSW

Children don't stay as children forever! As time progress, they get older and develop and mature into the men or women they are intended to be...or do they? Does time play a factor in their progression or does a parents' love and involvement hinder that progression?

Forty to fifty years ago, children were being raised in a world where mothers were "stay-at-home" mothers and less females were working being forced to raise their children. There was assistance by maternal and paternal grandparents in times of needs. However, it was more of a quiet and settled time where children were at home being raised by their mothers. Caring for children was easier as there was no internet, no social media, and no form of intervention. Instead, there was black and white television and children played outside. Families appeared to be united and helped each other out. There didn't appear to be any turmoil or issues as roles were being carried out. Big families got along and taught each other the values, principles and the importance of having a mother and a village attached to their upbringing. Mothers played the primary role of ensuring she was raising her children while the fathers had employment and supported the family financially. Their TIME was invested in all their children's upbringing!

What was the difference in parenting in years gone by versus parenting in today's world? What can we bring back from those years that was working and that we are doing incorrectly today? What is the missing link to affect today's children and what those children are missing? You guessed it...TIME!

Where's Mom?

Why is a mother spending time with her children so vital? How is it that giving birth to a child is not enough? You birthed them and delivered them into this world. Shouldn't this be enough?

One would say the comments previously made are...CRAZY right? If only it were that easy! Ironically, I can say giving birth is the easy part of the childhood process. Raising children especially as a single mother is one of the hardest things in life! Children don't come with instructions. It's more challenging when your own life hasn't been full of support, knowledge, help and vital information on how to raise a child. Where do you get the knowledge? How will you be able to raise a child on your own? I am here to tell you it can be achieved! You can do it! Is it easy? No...However, you can, you do it but it will always return to that one question about...Time! How much time do you have for your child or children? What are you willing to sacrifice in your life for time with your children?

TIME is another component to raising solid, competent, independent males and females. As I have said before, this is not easy to do! However, it can be done with the dedication you are willing to provide to your child and/or children. Hopefully, you will not sacrifice your children's time. You must be willing to sacrifice someone or something else. It is a matter of your decision making. Making choices for all, around what you provide and how much time you provide your children. Those decisions affect what happens in our lives, as well as, our children's lives. We are for the most part making day to day decisions on what we will do with our lives and our children. What we provide today to them, will more than likely be an indication of their outcome tomorrow.

This is not information that I am giving you just to write! It's a reality which has been confirmed! Children need their mothers! Mothers need to be mothers and put in their time! I didn't make up this rule! This is not my own personal inspirational wish for you although I want it to be. I want for all mothers in the world to raise their children. This is a harsh reality of what isn't happening in today's world! Women were made to be the carriers of children and then raising them (even if they are drug users or sick) Of course with the help and support of other people while being rehabilitated.

I'm not saying ALL women who have children will be able to raise them (some may die having them) but the likelihood of a child growing up in a less dysfunctional home will occur, if he/she is raised by his or her mother. You cannot negate the importance of a mother's role! There is no way around that! Am I saying if you don't get raised by your mother, a child's life, will be meaningless or unproductive or the likelihood is they will be in jail or repeat the history of what you did? NO...

However, I am saying there is a greater chance for those outcomes to happen. I do not wish this on anyone nor is it my desire for you to be unhappy, dysfunctional or even imprisoned in your world. My hopes and wishes are that as you are reading this book, you understand how YOUR time with your children is so important for their healthy adulthood. Your presence is KEY to their success! Your presence is needed all the time, so they can in turn provide a healthy and stable life for their own children.

Another key to this success in raising your children, is going against your comfort level. Raising children takes work which means you are not always feeling comfortable with the decisions you must make pertaining to their well-being. However, hang in there and be ready to be uncomfortable several times throughout their lives. There are going to be times where you won't want to put in the time, or to make decisions to influence their well-being or to just make them or yourself happy and it is ok! However, don't give up! Remember the goal of your role as the adult in the home. Remember not all decisions are going to feel good but ask yourself the question, (what is the outcome to this decision you are making?) Will any good come from it? Will my child learn from this decision and make the right decision? A little effort will bring great outcomes. Time means effort and both are relative to what your child needs.

History will repeat itself, and it will continue repeating itself until the cycle is broken! Somewhere and somehow the vicious cycle has to be broken. Mom, it starts with YOU! Put in the time and effort that comes with child bearing. It needs to be done and correctly to break the cycle of children feeling alone and rejected; hence finding a path that may get them into trouble as they seek to fill the void.

Those choices of stealing, replacing their lives with gang members, being jailed and possibly even killing, at such a young age can be eliminated if there is intervention! Let's be honest with ourselves and note what is happening around the world is real! This is happening today in your neighborhood, city or country! Youth today are destroying themselves and others because they were not raised at home by their mother!

The madness has to stop, and it starts with you as their mother! There is a cry for help by these children at a very young age to be given a chance at life for what lays ahead in the future... It starts with you, the female; the mother who was provided with a chance to pass along to your child, the foundation, the skills, the love, the support EVERY child deserves at birth! I'm not saying a father's role is not important as it definitely is; however, a father is who has been known to be the "breadwinner." A man is not made biologically to bear children and have the bond which starts with inception. He is important in a child's life, but he is not the "mother." The mother has to be primarily involved in his/her child's life! This information is being disseminated for those females who are not putting in the appropriate amount of time in their children's lives. This is for those mothers who think they cannot raise their children because of...WHATEVER, the reasons are! Time is of the essence...

CHAPTER V:
Adolescence

Jannette Ramos, MSW

You were blessed with having a child, and it is your responsibility to love and provide your child with all of the basics he or she needs to have! To be loved, cared for and given the time and the attention a child and youth so need is what should be your priority! They remain your responsibility for the first 18 years by law! They don't come into this world to be given to a system, to an aunt, an uncle, or a friend... They are your responsibility! It is your job as a mother whether you were single or not, to put valuable time into your children's lives! Their own lives depend on it!

Think about your friends, family members, neighbors or just stories you hear or know about where mothers haven't been raising their children. How are their lives, their children's lives and all of the lives involved in this? What used to be a grandmother's assistance, stepping in to be a support in a trusted way to help raise a child 40 or 50 years ago, is not what children appreciate or accept today. Unless one's mother passes away from an illness or giving birth to a child, children upon becoming young adults are not forgiving! The lack of parenting will affect the way your child will develop into his or her adult being. Although having a family member assisting by stepping in and trying to replace a mother, can and is valuable, the role of a mother cannot be substituted! Through no fault of anyone, children want to feel loved, acknowledged and assume their identity.

A relationship that only a mother can provide them is one which cannot be explained, but it is one that has a critical impact on a child's decision making! Children need their mothers! The decisions you make as a mother will convey into your children's lives. How

Where's Mom?

can change occur? It has to start within you. You have to raise your children the best way YOU know how so they can enjoy better opportunities in life. Otherwise, many of the outcomes occurring in the world will remain in effect, and negative change will continue in today's society. There is a deep correlation between these NEGATIVE behaviors and a lack of mothering. Wake up and be mothers for the sake of a better world!

My children's adolescence has been one of my favorite times in my life! I watched my children growing into the fine men as would be expected for a mother who put in the vital necessary time with her children! Adolescence... This is a time many avoid, dislike or stay away. They say it is the toughest times in their children's lives. For me, it was a beautiful time.

What made my journey with them different? I was part of everything they did! I made it my business to be nosy, to be involved and to be around them daily. I asked questions, I probed, I intervened to help, to support and to engage with them. I wrapped myself in their matters and was consumed with anything and everything they did! Why? Because they were my children and I needed to know what was going on in their lives! I had to be a witness to daily events, concerns, and happy adventures. It was important to know they were OK.

My job was to parent them and by being truly there (not merely taking space) I was able to gain knowledge of what each child was enduring in his life. If It was something that needed immediate attention, it was resolved! There was no grass growing under my feet when it came to immediately handling any situations that had to do with either of them. The matter was handled as best and positive as it could be. Children are like sponges and absorb all you do and how you handle situations as they arise. I was always able to handle any situation without compromising my integrity or placing any one of us in danger, to bring comfort and peace...no matter what the situation was.

I'm not saying I was perfect or that every decision was the correct decision. However, I'm saying I made decisions to ensure we were treated in a respectful way. I enjoyed a peaceful life, and that's what I've vowed I would give my children. All our lives needed and depended on it. I knew my children would become youth and then, grown men. I had to model a balanced way of living but more importantly, I had to be there every day to show them the way to be! I needed them to know life is not always easy, but they could handle anything that came their way which would make the difference between a good or a good outcome. Let's face it; children behave the way they see their parents behaving. It is important as parents we show them calm and peaceful behavior. We reap what we sow!

Society seems to have a hard time with teens today! They seem to think teenagers are disrespectful, ignorant males or females who don't care or give an "F" about anyone around them. This is not true! Adolescence is a challenging time for young males and females, especially today. They are bombarded by many stresses to manage and the last thing they need

Where's Mom?

is to be raising themselves or be raised by a relative! Adolescence is a rough time, with peer pressure, puberty and hormones, making friends, establishing who you are and what you want to do with your life.

Let's think about that for a minute! You have so much going on in your life as a teenager that can be and is confusing. Now add to it that you don't have your mother there to provide you with unconditional love and guidance. Explosion of emotions!!! And if they turn off their own emotions, displaying a flat affect to what they are experiencing, they are causing havoc for tomorrow! They are trying to process all the emotions that have built up over the years! Adolescent males and females are people too! They don't want or wish to be angry or rebellious. They desire what everyone else wants and should receive in their lives... A healthy upbringing! A world full of attention, direction, guidance, support and presence.

These kids are not born angry or antisocial! They don't just become what they become because they are bad humans. Unfortunately, their home life and lack of parenting is what causes them to react negatively. Those negative behaviors are going to be noticed. Remember acting out negatively to get attention, is better than no attention. If a mother took the time to be a part of their lives, certain negative behaviors would not occur! To be a part of what your child is doing daily will be manifested through their day-to-day actions.

On the other hand, I do need to express that I understand one cannot be with your child or children all the time; I get it! It is impossible, of course, even unhealthy to be with your child all the time. But what I am saying is that being mother comes with both positive and negative moments. Behaviors are behaviors whether they are positive or negative. Children do not come with instructions, but it is our job to make sure as parents and especially as mothers that we are involved and in tune in with what our children do day in and day out! It is our responsibility and it is our number one priority to be a responsible parent so that the odds of our children becoming sane, functional, and healthy adults are high! I don't pretend to know everything about child rearing or being a perfect parent. No parent is perfect and we are a work in progress.

There's no way to be a perfect mother, however, there are a million ways to be a good one. Be the best possible mother you can be! Put in your time with your child and make it your business to get into their business, so you know what goes on in their lives! They need it! Their lives depend on it! We think the adolescent stage is one where we must refrain from becoming involved and that is far from the truth! They need your involvement! They want you to ask questions and know what goes on in their lives. Why wouldn't you want to know? Working long hours, two jobs, don't care, on drugs, not focused, not important to you are examples of what happens to parents when they are unaware of what is going on in their child's lives. This is your child and you need and should know what happens to them! The cycle has to be broken!

You need to care and understand children don't ask to be here and have "no fault" for the mistakes or negative decisions we make! What they want to know is you are THERE for them and care what happens to them! Especially when they reach their teenage years! It doesn't get easier for you or them! It gets harder, and their future will become a by-product of what they have endured in their own lives!

As I stated earlier in the book, even a parent providing negative attention is better than no attention. Negative attention or negative behaviors provided by a mother, give a youth the opportunity to see and make decisions for themselves. Even if it means they will follow in their mother's footsteps! At least they have been given a choice, which is better than not being given any chance at all! Give a youth the option to make the choice of wanting to follow in her/his mother's behaviors or not! We know what happens when they are not given this opportunity as teenagers. They act out, they steal, they get into criminal mischief, they become involved in gangs to provide the missing family, they engage in drug activity, and they become bitter, torn and scared!

They don't ask for this! They want to have a normal like everyone else. They want to have positive relationships with others and be a part of society! They want to feel important and productive in their lives. They want peace and tranquility in their lives! They want to be sane and normal! Although all home lives may not be equally normal and/or may even be dysfunctional, when you provide a mother who children see when they come into the world as their safety net...the risks will be less for these behaviors to occur. This has to be the focus so we save our youth and give them a better life in this world! It has to start from you! It's your turn to be a mother... for the sake of tomorrow's adults.

No amount of money in the world is worth subjecting your children to a life of turmoil, pain, resentment, sadness and challenges in adulthood! It's not the money that matters (although we need to raise children) it's the time you spend with your offspring; the dedication that as mothers we are required to provide our youth. Yes, in today's society if you don't work, you don't eat. I understand that as a mother in today's society you have to be able to work and it's ok. The main thing is to have a plan in place for your children's needs. In addition, all these needs must be met in a balanced form. Quality time has to be spent with your children even if you have to work either because you are raising them alone, or there's not enough money for paying your expenses or whatever the reasons are. Spending time with your children needs to happen frequently or you will get negative attention because you are not there with your children. Providing your time to your child is vital, more vital than gifts, presents or materialistic things. What will count in the long run is if you are dedicating your time to your children.

CHAPTER VI:
Lifelong Memories

Jannette Ramos, MSW

Children don't remain little or young forever. It's nice and comforting to know what they will and should be provided day in and day out are memories... Lifelong memories! What a concept to know and appreciate! What beauty it is to have memories so that each time we want to revert back to a moment in time, we are allowed to do so via a video camera, pictures and our own pictures of moment retention! Children bring so much energy and passion into our lives, we cannot catch every moment or we can try to catch those moments. However, we know it is impossible to grasp all moments of our children's lives but what if we could? How phenomenal would that be?

What memories do you have or can you remember about your children's lives? Too much to remember? Unfortunately, we cannot remember everything and sometimes our vision is cluttered or unclear and we only remember clips or snaps of one event or a few events that were important in ours and in their lives! I'm sure if you had a scenario with two participants, each person would tell the story a little differently or omit a piece of the story! It's what we as individuals remember and there isn't a right or wrong answer. The point is that when we have these snaps or moments of memory, we either embrace those memories or we want to forget them.

Let's think about your memories as it relates to your children. Children are always building memories in their lives in hopes of those memories being good ones! Their memories of their raising should be pleasant for most of their upbringing. They shouldn't have negative memories of their mother to be replayed or remembered. It's unhealthy and it affects them as children and carries into their adulthood. Memories being stored in the brain should be a reflection of the daily activities and day-to-day living that mold a child into their inner person! They carry those memories for as long as they live! It is reality! What lifelong memories do you have of your child? Are there many of them? If not, why is that so? What can you recall about your memories with your child or children? Are they positive or negative memories?

Making lifelong memories is something we need to make happen in our lives regularly and it's not happening if we are not building them regularly! How do we get there? Well, I can tell you we don't get there if we are not present or hardly there! I have made that point clear. We have to make those memories with our children, and it doesn't happen on its own. We have to ensure to build positive memories as building negative-ones is like never building any because you were not there to do so! The outcome of negativity is still there. Imagine your childhood and all the memories you have stored within you and how does it make you feel? Happy, sad or angry? What would you have done to change the negative feelings? Probably nothing because it wasn't your fault!

You were a child who needed to be surrounded by a positive female/mother who would nurture, guide and protect you! It wasn't your place as a child to be responsible for certain things that took place around you. You were developing, existing and slowly finding out who you were going to become. Your job is to be a kid; an innocent child and not have any adult responsibilities. Every child wants lifelong memories. Well, it's time and interaction which provides the environment to be able to build those memories. To be able to relive any positive memories with all that, one does with their own child is priceless! Money cannot buy the memories you wish you had with your child; memories that will carry-on for the rest of their lives!

Time waits for no man or woman and before one knows it, we will have aged and so will our children! The best thing in the world that we can't buy with money is our children's respect. Some of that respect come from the positive intimate relationship you gain solely from spending and making those memories with them. Nothing in life is free and neither is their respect for you, if you haven't earned it! You have to invest your time into your child. You hope it is enough or there was enough invested for it to be reciprocated. It is a harsh reality to recognize our children would not respect us on the basis of what could have been avoided, if the relationship was developed on a secure foundation. This is a foundation which entails nurturing and love throughout the child's life unconditionally!

Money, fame or anything else that you can think of can't replace the mourning a male or female has because they do not possess lifelong memories with the woman who carried him/her in her womb for nine months. It is unexplainable the slew of emotions children carry within them during their lives and would replace for the love of their mother! If not for the mere fact of feeling a sense of belonging but to receive a better chance in society, we owe it to our children to provide them a chance at life with an opportunity to succeed. A chance to be able to

Where's Mom?

provide generations and generations of lifelong memories; it's what we were brought into this life for.

CHAPTER VII:
Solitude Effects

What will your life set out to be if you don't raise your child or children? A life of some misery for them and for yourself! For them; a world of many mistakes, some crime involvement and disaster! Look at the world around you today! Many of the violent acts of crime are being committed by the adults of 25 years of age and younger. This could've easily been prevented, had you the mother raised your child! Yes, not raising your child increases the likelihood of them living and leading a life that can ultimately destroy them. They will either end up in prison, in dysfunctional relationships, having a life with many mistakes or negative decisions due to the lack of your presence.

You have basically chosen your child's fate by making the decision not to raise them on your own! You have and are contributing to their acts by not providing your child with the time and attention that they deserve and need! Your presence and time matter in a child's life! Without you, there is no productive sane life! Is that what you signed up for when you wanted to be a mother? With every decision comes consequences and you except them upon knowing that you didn't put in your time in your child's life! These young adults don't choose or most don't choose a life that is criminally based! They are conditioned to be what they become on the lacking in their lives! Lack of love, time, attention, support, guidance, direction, communication, patience, understanding, acceptance, absence, teaching, education, lack of finances etc. has thrown them out to the wolves, to fend for themselves. All of these makes your child suffer to the point where the lack manifests in other forms or fashion!

Where's Mom?

Here's an example, when a child acts out in our eyes or in general, what is causing, he or she to do so? Is it to get on your nerves? Is it because he or she cannot control it or could simply be that negative behaviors are better than no behaviors as the child now gains the adults attention? Young children need your attention! They need to know they matter, that you care about them and everything that happens to them. This is not 'rocket science folks" and it's just that simple! Devote the time to your child, so they display normal behaviors because children don't want to act out. They don't wake up saying they're going to get on their mother's nerves or want to cause you heartache or pain! They simply want to be acknowledged and given attention! It's how humans are wired to be!

We are sending our children out to be delinquents of tomorrow when we don't provide them with what they are due! Does it really take or a deep understanding to comprehend this simple concept? I don't think it does! What I am stating is crystal clear... You're important in your child's life and if you aren't there, he/she will pay the consequences in one way or another! I'm not saying he or she will turn out to be a criminal, a murderer, or their life will be such a disastrous one that they will not be able to function in society. But what I am saying is the lack of parenting will display in some negative behaviors as they become adults and carry with them throughout their entire lives. Some behaviors will be more severe in some than others. Remember, you're the important piece of the puzzle.

Don't you want to know that when you pass on, your child or children are in the best possible state of mind they can be? Don't you want to know they are financially and emotionally successful? Ultimately, isn't that what all parents want for their children? Once more, I'm not saying raising children is an easy job but it is doable. You made this decision when you decided to give birth to children. I know for a fact as I raised two children on my own; and thinking back to all the trials and hurdles that came my way, I wouldn't have done it any other way!

These children were mine to raise until they were capable to do it for themselves and even still, my time is available for them anytime! Let's face it; 18 years is just a number that someone made up in society to distinguish the child becoming an adult! I believe children at 18 years of age are still growing and in great need of their mother and direction. 18 years is not a magical number where life becomes different in thought process or decisions are thoroughly made correctly. It's still a time in these young adults that have fear, doubt, neediness and require direction. However, at least if you have delivered them to these years then you have made a crucial difference. This is what truly matters. Anything after 18 years will be trial and errors on their part as they have to make mistakes in their lives. This is the path of mankind. Hang in there in the meantime and see what wonders happen in the world as a result of your motherly role.

CHAPTER VIII:
Rewards

What can I say about rewards? Children are the best reward we as parents can be given. They are a gift from God! They have been provided to us to make our lives matter and without them, our lives would be boring, senseless, without meaning, and non-fruitful!

Children bring us so much joy. There is no other joy that compares to the lifelong memories we build with our children Nothing compares to the wonders that come from raising your kids! How incredible is it that you can have a part of you to carry on after you are gone?

What a good feeling to know that you have been there every step of the way! There is no greater feeling to know your child has become that adult that you have dreamt for them to become. You did it! Your sacrifices paid off; you can finally reap the benefits from your investment! Isn't that the best? You couldn't be any prouder! Your son or daughter has become the man or woman that he/she was destined to become after all your hard work!

The time has come to see them fly and exceed all expectations! Your child, your prince or princess will be sailing off to make a positive difference in the world because you undertook your job as a mother! You didn't give up! You defied all the odds that said you couldn't raise them regardless of where they were being raised or how much money you had or did not have! What is a better reward?

You'll be able to count on your children as they counted on you for all those years for any thing you're going to need help with because you put in your time!

Where's Mom?

The best thing to ensure you raise your children well is to give:

- Time
- Energy
- Attention
- Guidance
- Love
- Praise
- Encouragement

and to provide a safe environment using support including taking time to care for yourself.

But ultimately raise your children because this decision to put in the time will give you the best rewards in the world. The feeling of accomplishment even though it was a long and tough road and you stuck through all the bad and the good, is a feeling which allows you to conquer the world. It provides the ability to stand proud wherever you go and no one can say anything to you negatively about your children as you did it!

You parented the best way you could in the most positive and loving way possible. Making it well worth the sacrifice to see your children be successful in life! It all starts with the foundation you provide by parenting your child even when you are faced with obstacles you didn't think you could overcome. You resisted all the temptations of walking away or abandoning your child when things went wrong and when times were tough.

You believed in yourself to know the situation would get better and the world would not always feel like you were weighed down by it. You managed at times to cry, be sad, angry, happy, anxious, scared, surprised, tired and in pain, but you survived it! You didn't give up!!! You persevered! You pushed forward! You had hope!!! No amount of money in the world can pay for that feeling of success.

CHAPTER IX:
Second Chance

Everyone deserves a second chance in life as we all have problems in life and there is no perfect person. Life is not easy, and it wasn't meant to be! That's the way it is whether you are rich or poor! Problems do not discriminate! What problems do is feed on those who haven't been able to cope with day-to-day living and haven't taught to grab their problems by the ball horn and tackle them effectively.

I do believe one's upbringing plays a vivid and vital role in how we as adults solve problems. Some people take a path that leads them to use drugs or indulge in heavy drinking, being involved in criminal mischief, and some have mental health issues. One or any combination of these can end up with parents and children being separated. Not being able to cope with a problem, which usually is not going to be there very long, that we cannot control and is out of our hands, is merely called "worrying."

With time, worrying only intensifies the problems at hand. We have to find ways to eliminate or reduce how much worrying we do as a parent. Life is full of problems; it's how we handle the situation that matters.

With that being said, we make mistakes as parents and sometimes we do things because of what life has thrown at us at that particular time. However, we have a second chance to make things better and correct our mistakes. No matter how many mistakes you make as a parent, you cannot give up as you may not get another opportunity to fix your mistakes.

Where's Mom?

You have to fix your relationship with your child. If you do not have a relationship with your child ask yourself the question, why not? Is it for the mere fact at one point in your life you couldn't take care of him or her and you decided to give up totally? Who said you had to give up totally? Society? Your mother? Mourning on your past mistakes and faults? Who decides that after making a mistake with your child, you do not have the opportunity to make it up?

Yes, time is ticking and your children are maturing, however, you still have the opportunity to make matters right! You owe it to your child and to yourself. As human beings, nobody is perfect and we will continue to make mistakes, but the biggest MISTAKE is not working to have your child give you a second chance to build a relationship with them. This is your responsibility; not your children's responsibility. They didn't make the mistake; you did! While you have time to make up for your mistake; the problem is you don't have much time.

Children grow up quickly and depending on what stage in life you are in, will determine the type of relationship and the outcome you will have with your child.

Mistakes are made, and people deserve a second chance. How is that accomplished?

First, you have to be willing to admit you made a mistake; accept it, own up to it and acknowledge YOU made the mistake. It means placing your pride, honor, or any type of emotion that you have to the side. Removing that emotion or set of emotions keeping you from getting to the outcome; which is your child. This also means forgiving yourself for the past and the mistakes you made.

Second, seek to correct your mistake by figuring out what you will do differently now. You have a lot of work to do, and it won't be easy.

Third, make contact with the child who has been out of your life for however long and mend that relationship!

Who cares what took place in the past that you can dwell on and feel bad about! There are going to be memories that may hurt you forever. However, it is never too late to establish a relationship with your child so long as you don't wait too long and it's too late!

Remember children start to formulate their own opinions and feelings as they grow older. They will piece together what happened to them in their life. Although you haven't been there for them, you still have an opportunity to make up for that lost time! How you choose to do it, is up to you.

However, it is vital that you re-establish a relationship with your child. Even if you don't have the best relationship, you hopefully can salvage some part of your relationship. I'm not saying it's going to be easy. In fact, it's going to be more difficult depending on their ages. You could get away with establishing a relationship with a young child whose brain development has not been fully attained. However, for those preteens and teens, you'll have a

Where's Mom?

long explanation as to why you were not in their life. Even after your explanation, you will have to be putting in exactly what we've been talking about throughout this book...TIME!

You will have to rebuild what's been broken, which is dependent on the amount of time you put into your relationship. This is a selfless act on your part, Remember, although it's not easy; you can do it. You have to recognize the harsh reality of what your absence has done to your child. Let me be clear that absence means you will have to put in hard work to mend this relationship!

Are you willing to do that? Are you willing to have situations where your child will reprimand you for those times that you weren't there? To be spoken to harshly and to be yelled at? For your child to tell you they don't love you; they don't want you in their life? Or, you're a failure because you may not have tried hard enough? Or, you didn't care about them; you don't love them? Or, they feel nothing for you because you weren't around?

These are the kinds of questions you need to ask yourself and be prepared to talk about. You returning will reopen a wound that's been deeply imbedded for several years. A wound that's been covered and attempted to be nurtured by another adult. By someone else; a grandmother, a family friend, an aunt, an uncle, a foster parent, etc.

This is a consequence of being an absent mother for a long time. You may be able to have a second chance, but it may not come easily. You'll have to be prepared to cry, to be angry, to be anxious, to be in pain, to be embarrassed, to be empathetic and sympathetic, but most importantly, you have to be prepared, to be HONEST about what happened.

Every child in this world wants the truth about their past and their upbringing. They want to know how they were brought into this world and how or what went wrong that prompted them to go into another person's care! Your ability to share honest and truthful information to your child so he or she can understand and accept or not accept what transpired in their lives is extremely important. Acknowledge your mistakes and take ownership of them! Accept there are no perfect human beings in the world.

FORGIVE YOURSELF.
ASK YOUR CHILD FOR FORGIVENESS.

Do your part to make amends for what was broken. Do it before it is too late and your children grow up. You have the ability to have another chance with your child if you really want it. You have a better chance of gaining a relationship and mending those wounds your child sustained throughout the years that he or she was living without you!

Are you willing to go through this pain for the sake of your child? I would hope the answer is "YES", so each of you can resume a normal life or as normal as possible! Are you going to be the mother that your child has an unbroken bond with, or will you be the mother whose child is asking "Where's mom?"

CHAPTER X:
Final Thoughts
Take Care of Yourself

If you are thinking that raising children is an easy task, it is not! However, there are a variety of resources that can help you in your toughest times. You may find assistance from others including, family support, friends, neighbors and, in today's times; technology, books, videos, parenting support groups, etc. These can assist you when things go wrong and you feel you cannot parent your child or you are having a difficult time.

As a single parent, you need time for yourself to be an effective parent. Children have a tendency to drain us. You will need to discover ways to be recharged. As a mother, seek all the necessary resources, so you don't burn yourself out. You do not want to be making negative decisions and possibly acting in a negative fashion affecting your children.

Recognize that although parenting is tough, it's what we have been positioned to do for our children. I am not saying you need to be slaving to a child's everyday needs. After all, you are human and need to take care of yourself. Find ways of balancing your time between being a good mother and taking care of yourself. How are you going to be a better parent if you don't take care of yourself? What types of things can you do to take care of you on a day-to-day basis?

Here are a few things that you could do when you feel you need a break from your child or children and remain in your comfort zone. Smile, pray, interact with other individuals, meditate, read a book, exercise, meaning any form of exercise such as bike riding, aerobics class, strength training, stretching, yoga, Pilates, whatever is comfortable for you, sleep (but please have someone watch your child while you sleep), cook, bake, sew, go shopping, get your hair done, your face done via makeup or facial or both, a body massage, visit a friend, take a vacation (leaving someone to care for your child), have a glass of wine or your favorite drink, volunteer your time, watch a movie, create an invention, write a book, be thankful for your life, remain in the present, and remember nothing stays the same whether it's bad or good.

This may not be the case often but when it does come your way, appreciate it and take advantage of it. If you still require ways on how to parent or don't understand certain things in your child's life, read up on it, Google it, YouTube it, seek a group on parenting tips, etc. Know your life will not remain the same each and every day. Things will get better especially when you feel things are bad or are not going your way!

Parenting does get better with time. Know you were made to be a parent and its the best thing as human beings that we can provide for our offspring.

Be the best parent you were made to be! You owe it to yourself and your children.

Best of luck in parenting mom!

RESOURCES

Parenting Website
www.connectedfamilies.org

You Tube
Best parenting tips

Online Parenting Tips
www.theparenthelpcenter.com/parentsupport

Books
The best parenting tips for parents

Blogs
www.thesinglemomjourney.com

www.ingramcontent.com/pod-product-compliance
Lightning Source LLC
Chambersburg PA
CBHW051133160426
43195CB00014B/2456